Original title:
Heartfelt Steps

Copyright © 2024 Swan Charm
All rights reserved.

Author: Paula Raudsepp
ISBN HARDBACK: 978-9916-89-742-3
ISBN PAPERBACK: 978-9916-89-743-0
ISBN EBOOK: 978-9916-89-744-7

The Path of Tender Whispers

In quietude, the spirit breathes,
Soft murmurs weave through the trees.
Each leaf a prayer, gentle and bright,
Guiding hearts toward the light.

With every step, the soul unfolds,
Stories of grace in whispers told.
The starry sky above ignites,
A dance of faith in sacred nights.

In stillness, love begins to flow,
Upon the path, the heart shall grow.
Each sigh a song, profound and wise,
Illuminates the darkest skies.

With every heartbeat, hope revived,
In tender moments, we survive.
Hand in hand, we walk as one,
Embraced by love, under the sun.

In the garden where spirits meet,
Every footfall, a heartfelt beat.
Whispers echo, soft and clear,
In sacred spaces, love draws near.

Footfalls on Sacred Ground

With humble hearts, we tread light,
On sacred ground, beneath the night.
Each step a prayer, a silent vow,
In awe of grace, we bend and bow.

The earth does sing beneath our feet,
In nature's choir, our souls repeat.
Glimmers of hope in every sound,
As we make peace on sacred ground.

In twilight's glow, we seek and find,
The threads of love, forever twined.
With open hearts, we learn to stand,
As one with life, we join the band.

With every whisper of the breeze,
The spirit calls us to our knees.
We gather close, in faith profound,
United here on sacred ground.

Echoes of the Soul's Journey

In the stillness, echoes rise,
Reflections dance in the skies.
The journey calls, both near and far,
Guided gently by the star.

Through trials faced and joys embraced,
The soul embarks, love interlaced.
Each moment carved, each lesson learned,
In sacred fires, our hearts are burned.

Through valleys deep and mountains high,
We walk the path, with spirits nigh.
Each step a note in a timeless song,
Together journeying, where we belong.

In whispers soft, the truth we glean,
In every heartbeat, grace is seen.
The soul's journey, a tapestry bright,
Woven with love, bathed in light.

Pilgrimage of the Loving Spirit

Upon a road both worn and new,
We walk with faith, our spirits true.
In every stride, love holds us near,
A pilgrimage, where none must fear.

Through sacred lands, where shadows fade,
We honor all the love displayed.
With open hands and hearts set free,
We find our place in unity.

With every tear that marks the way,
We shed the past, embrace the day.
Each moment tender, sweet, and grand,
In the loving spirit, we firmly stand.

With trust as our guiding star,
We travel on, no dream too far.
Together, hearts as one shall rise,
In the stillness of the skies.

Lifting Our Souls with Every Step

With every footfall on this blessed land,
We rise together, hand in hand.
In whispers soft, the spirit sings,
Through trials faced, our faith takes wings.

The dawn breaks bright, a promise clear,
In shadows cast, we hold no fear.
Each moment graced by Heaven's light,
We tread the path, guided by right.

With hearts ablaze, we search for grace,
In every smile, in every place.
The love we share, a sacred bond,
In unity, we journey on.

The sacred ground beneath our feet,
In prayerful steps, we are complete.
We lift our souls with every breath,
Embracing life, conquering death.

O'er hills and valleys, onward we stride,
In faith and hope, forever our guide.
Together, we shall rise above,
Each step a testament of love.

The Oasis of Faith

In the quiet grove, where the stillness dwells,
The heart finds peace, as the spirit swells.
With every prayer, the waters flow,
An oasis blooms, where grace will grow.

Through barren lands, we seek the light,
In shadows cast, we find our sight.
With open hands, we gather near,
The sacred gift of hope appears.

Beneath the stars, our dreams take flight,
In cosmic dance, we feel the might.
The universe sings a soothing tune,
In still of night, beneath the moon.

Together we stand, strong and tall,
A family forged, the greatest call.
In love and faith, we intertwine,
An oasis found, perfectly divine.

As seasons change, our roots run deep,
In trust we walk, in faith we leap.
The journey's long, yet spirits soar,
In this haven, we're forever more.

Walking Among the Saints

In holiness we find our way,
Amidst the light of every day.
With every step, we honor those,
Whose faith and love forever glows.

They walked this earth with tender grace,
Their stories weave through time and space.
With hearts so bold, they paved the way,
Guiding us through night and day.

Each saint a beacon, shining bright,
In darkest hours, they are our light.
We lift our voices, sing their song,
In unity we all belong.

Their whispers echo through the air,
In every prayer, we feel them there.
With every choice, we seek to shine,
And emulate their love divine.

As we walk on, their spirits guide,
In sacred strength, we will abide.
Each step a tribute, hand in hand,
Together we stand, a faithful band.

Echoes of Celestial Guidance

In dawn's embrace, we hear the call,
The echoes rise, embracing all.
Through gentle winds, the whispers flow,
Guiding our hearts, wherever we go.

The stars above, a sacred sign,
In cosmic dance, their light intertwines.
With every sigh, they lead the way,
Through trials faced, they help us stay.

Around us swirl the angels' grace,
Each moment blessed, our spirits trace.
In silent prayer, we seek the peace,
As faith and love shall never cease.

With open eyes, we see the signs,
The path ahead in sacred lines.
As echoes linger, we find our track,
In trust we march, no looking back.

In every heart, a guiding light,
We journey forth from dark to bright.
Together in faith, we shall unite,
In echoes of love, we find our might.

Echoes of Divine Whispers

In the stillness, voices blend,
Carried softly on the breeze,
Guiding hearts to the holy end,
Filling souls with sacred ease.

Through the night, a candle glows,
Illuminating paths unknown,
In its light, the Spirit flows,
A connection, two hearts sewn.

With each prayer, a echo grows,
Vibrations of love pure and bright,
In the silence, grace bestows,
A tapestry woven with light.

Listen well, the wisdom speaks,
In daily moments, find the call,
In the humble, the exalted seeks,
With open hearts, we shall not fall.

Let the whispers guide our way,
Through the darkness into dawn,
In the grace of a new day,
A promise made, we carry on.

Graceful Ascent to the Heavens

Like a bird upon the wing,
Soaring high in skies so wide,
Echoing the songs we sing,
As we follow, hearts abide.

With each step, the world unfolds,
In the journey, truths refine,
In the warmth of love it holds,
We ascend, the stars align.

Through the trials, faith remains,
A beacon in the depths of night,
In our hearts, eternal flames,
Turning darkness into light.

In the silence, prayers take flight,
Carried forth on winds of grace,
In the stillness, find the might,
To embrace our sacred place.

With each moment, rise and shine,
In the glory of His name,
In the dance, we intertwine,
Graceful steps, a holy flame.

Where Spirit Meets Soil

In the garden, blessings flow,
Life awakened, roots embrace,
In the soil, seeds softly sow,
Each a story, sacred space.

From the earth, to sky we rise,
Nature's hymn, a vibrant song,
In the heartbeat of the skies,
Where we find we all belong.

With the rain, a gentle kiss,
Nourishing the bonds we share,
In the darkness, find the bliss,
In the soil, love's tender care.

Every flower tells a tale,
Of hope's pursuit beneath the sun,
In the whispers, never pale,
United, we are all as one.

In the twilight, shadows blend,
Filling hearts with endless grace,
From the soil, our journeys wend,
Where spirit finds its rightful place.

A Tapestry of Sacred Strides

In every step, a prayer unfolds,
Threads of faith woven tight,
In the journey, wisdom holds,
A sacred dance in morning light.

Each encounter, a stitch embraced,
In the fabric of our days,
Finding beauty, love interlaced,
In the myriad of His ways.

Through the valleys, mountains high,
We traverse with hearts awake,
In the whispers of the sky,
A connection that none can break.

With a vision, united we stand,
In the tapestry, one and all,
Every heartbeat, a guiding hand,
In His presence, we will not fall.

So let us walk along this path,
With humility, grace, and pride,
In our souls, the aftermath,
A tapestry woven, love inside.

Reaching for the Light

In shadows deep, we yearn to see,
The gentle glow that sets us free.
With hands outstretched, we seek the grace,
To find our way in sacred space.

Through trials faced, our spirits rise,
In every tear, a promise lies.
Together, hearts in faith unite,
For love's embrace, we reach the light.

Each step we take is paved in hope,
With every prayer, we learn to cope.
In whispers soft, the truth resounds,
In faith's embrace, our purpose found.

The dawn will break, the night will fade,
In every heart, His love displayed.
With open minds, we chase the bright,
Together bound, we reach the light.

With every breath, His Word we claim,
In joy and peace, we praise His name.
For in our hearts, He shines so bright,
Forevermore, we seek the light.

Stones Beneath Our Feet

Along the path, the stones await,
Each one a lesson, each one a fate.
With every step, we learn and grow,
In trials met, His love we know.

The weary wanderers we become,
Yet through each trial, we find our home.
For burdens shared and faith aligned,
In every stone, His love defined.

The road is long, the journey steep,
Yet in His arms, our hearts to keep.
With stones beneath, we walk in trust,
For in His strength, we rise robust.

In moments dark, we lift our eyes,
To find the truth beyond the lies.
Each stone a marker of our fight,
Together strong, we bear the night.

So let us walk with heads held high,
With faith our guide, we'll touch the sky.
Embrace the stones, for they will teach,
In every step, His love we reach.

The Divine Within Our Stride

In every stride, divinity flows,
Each heartbeat whispers, love bestows.
We carry grace in every leap,
Awakening souls from their sleep.

With open hearts, we journey wide,
In unity, we walk, abide.
For every soul has its own song,
Together lifting all the throng.

The spirit guides with gentle hand,
In every moment, we take a stand.
For in our hearts, His truths reside,
Reflecting light with every stride.

In trials met, our faith ignites,
A beacon bright in darkest nights.
With strength renewed, we face the tide,
For there's a spark, the divine, inside.

Let love and kindness lead the way,
As we embrace each brand-new day.
In every step, His grace shall bide,
Celebrating life with joyful stride.

Heaven's Pathway Unfolds

On Heaven's path, our spirits soar,
With every step, we seek for more.
The light ahead, a guiding star,
In love and peace, we journey far.

Through valleys low, and mountains tall,
In every struggle, we hear His call.
For in the silence, His voice abides,
In faith and hope, our heart resides.

As blossoms bloom along the road,
We carry forth each sacred load.
The pathway clear, the skies are bright,
In every soul, His love ignites.

With open hands and grateful hearts,
In living faith, each life imparts.
The journey blessed, in trust we fold,
With every step, Heaven's tale told.

So let us walk, unwavering still,
With faith our guide, we're bound to fill.
For on this path, His grace unfolds,
A story rich, as Heaven holds.

Steps Through the Valley of Shadows

In shadows deep, we tread the way,
Each footfall whispers, come what may.
With faith as light, our hearts do glow,
Through trials faced, we learn and grow.

Though darkness looms, we seek His grace,
A guiding hand, in every place.
The valley bends, yet hope remains,
In every sorrow, love sustains.

Lift up your eyes, where dawn is near,
In quiet strength, we cast our fear.
With every step, the path unfolds,
A promise kept, through ages told.

Let peace rain down from skies above,
In every heartbeat, feel His love.
From shadows cast to light so bright,
We walk by faith, in purest sight.

To valleys wide, we lose our chains,
In sacred trust, our spirit gains.
Embracing light, we find our home,
In shadows deep, we're never alone.

Faith's Footprint in the Sand

On golden shores, our journey starts,
With every step, we share our hearts.
The waves may rise, the winds may roar,
Yet in His love, we find much more.

Each grain of sand, a tale to tell,
Of struggles faced, and how we fell.
But footprints linger, side by side,
In storms of doubt, He is our guide.

When shadows loom and night is long,
We lift our voices, sing His song.
In every trial, we find His hand,
Together strong, we take our stand.

The ocean vast, a mirror clear,
Reflects the love that casts out fear.
Through ebb and flow, our hopes align,
In faith's embrace, our souls entwine.

With every wave, the past must fade,
Yet in our hearts, His path is laid.
So let us walk through night and day,
With faith's bright light to guide the way.

Echoes of the Ancients

In whispers soft, the ancients call,
Their voices rise, a guiding thrall.
Through history's veil, their wisdom cries,
With sacred truths that never dies.

From distant lands, their lessons flow,
In every heart, their seeds do sow.
In sunlit glades or hidden groves,
The echo speaks of love that roves.

We walk the path they forged with care,
Each step we take, a silent prayer.
For in their tales, we find our own,
A shared journey, we're not alone.

With every heartbeat, time bends near,
As ancient truths dissolve our fear.
In unity, our spirits rise,
Transcending realms, to touch the skies.

So heed the call, let wisdom reign,
In every loss, there's much to gain.
For in their echoes, we discover,
The sacred bond, each soul a brother.

Sacred Rhythms of Life

In every heartbeat, life unfolds,
A sacred rhythm, timeless, bold.
With dawn's embrace, the world awakes,
Each moment cherished, love remakes.

The dance of seasons, sun and rain,
In every joy, in every pain.
Resilience blooms, like flowers bright,
In nature's hand, we find our light.

From mountains high to oceans wide,
The pulse of life, forever tied.
In every creature, great and small,
A tapestry of love for all.

Let gratitude, our hearts inspire,
In sacred rhythms, we lift higher.
For in the stillness, wisdom flows,
A sacred song, the spirit knows.

So let us weave this life we share,
With threads of kindness, love, and care.
In sacred rhythms, find our peace,
Where every struggle finds release.

Crossing the Threshold of Grace

In silence, I arrive at the gate,
With whispers of faith, I contemplate.
Each step a prayer, each breath a sigh,
In this sacred space, I lift my eyes.

The light surrounds, a gentle embrace,
Washing my soul with mercy and grace.
A journey begun with humble plea,
In the heart's sanctuary, I am free.

With every heartbeat, love does unfold,
Stories of wisdom, silently told.
A path of thorns turns to fields of peace,
In the arms of the Divine, all burdens cease.

Time bows down, as I find my ground,
In the soft hush, His presence found.
Crossing the threshold, I feel reborn,
Into the light, the shadows are shorn.

Oh sweet grace, my guiding star,
From this moment on, I'll travel far.
In the embrace of the Holy light,
I walk this path, guided by right.

A Pilgrimage of the Heart

In the silence of dawn, my journey starts,
With faith as my compass, guiding hearts.
Each step a tribute, each mile a prayer,
Traversing the world, with love to share.

Mountains rise high, valleys dip low,
In every heartbeat, His presence flows.
The road winds onward, steep and wide,
With grace as my guide, I shall abide.

Beneath the weight of burdens I bear,
I find solace in moments bare.
The sacred whispers echo in the air,
As I walk this path, stripped of despair.

Every stranger I meet holds a piece,
Of God's vast love that brings me peace.
Together we rise, in unity strong,
A chorus of souls, singing a song.

At journey's end, I look back and see,
The countless blessings given to me.
With open arms, I embrace the part,
This pilgrimage of life, a sacred heart.

Glorious Ascent Toward Eternity

To the mountaintop, I soar on high,
With wings of hope, I touch the sky.
Each step a promise, each breath a song,
In the light of His love, I belong.

The path is narrow, steep is the climb,
Yet in His grace, I find no time.
With faith as my anchor, I rise with ease,
Toward the eternal, on bended knees.

In shadows that whisper of fear and doubt,
His light shines through, casting all out.
The summit awaits with joy untold,
A glimpse of the glory, a truth to behold.

Oh, to ascend where the angels sing,
In the heart of the heavens, my spirit takes wing.
With each rapture of love, I feel reborn,
In the glorious ascent, a new dawn is sworn.

Eternity beckons; I follow the call,
In the arms of His mercy, I shall not fall.
With stars as my guide in the night sky wide,
I journey onward, forever His bride.

The Echo of Solitary Steps

In the stillness, my footsteps hum,
A melody soft as the morning sun.
Each stride a hymn, each pause a grace,
In solitude, I find a sacred space.

The world fades away, a fleeting sound,
In quiet moments, His love is found.
A path of reverence, winding and deep,
Where secrets of the heart gently seep.

With each breath taken, I draw near,
To the whisper of hope, calm and clear.
Alone yet cherished, I feel His embrace,
In the echo of steps, I find my place.

Through valleys of silence, I wander long,
In the dance of shadows, I feel so strong.
For every solitude leads to connection,
Life's inner rhythm, a spiritual reflection.

The journey is deep; the path is mine,
With every heartbeat, His love divine.
In solitary moments, I hear my creed,
The echo of footsteps, the heart's true need.

Walking the Divine Labyrinth

In the maze of sacred thought,
Whispers of wisdom softly sought,
Guided by a holy light,
We tread upon the path of right.

With every turn, the soul is tested,
In quietude, the heart is rested,
Each step speaks of truth and grace,
In the labyrinth, we find our place.

The shadows flicker, hope prevails,
Through trials, love's hand never fails,
A journey cloaked in trials vast,
Finding solace in the past.

We climb the heights, we seek the fount,
In prayer, every soul does count,
The walls may close, yet faith expands,
In unity, we make our stands.

And as we walk the winding way,
With every dawn, we find our stay,
The heart rejoices, the spirit sings,
In the Divine, the promise springs.

The Call of the Infinite Journey

Beyond the stars, the journey calls,
Through ancient roads, the spirit sprawls,
With every heartbeat, we ascend,
To realms where love will never end.

Across the seas of time and fate,
In every moment, we contemplate,
The whispers of the unseen guide,
In trust, we step, with hearts open wide.

Mountains rise, and valleys fall,
Yet faith remains, it conquers all,
For in the quest, we find our truth,
A childlike heart, a timeless youth.

The winds may shift, the skies may storm,
In every challenge, we are reborn,
With wisdom drawn from trials faced,
Through love's embrace, we've interlaced.

We heed the call with reverent stride,
In every heartbeat, spirit's guide,
The journey's vast, yet love is near,
In grace, we wander without fear.

Steps of the Believer

With faith as light, we start our trek,
In shadows deep, we find our neck,
Each step we take is steeped in prayer,
In every moment, love we share.

The road may twist, the night may fall,
Yet in the silence, we hear the call,
Eager footsteps on sacred ground,
In our hearts, His purpose found.

As rivers flow to meet the sea,
Our souls unite in harmony,
Through trials faced and burdens borne,
In the embrace, we are reborn.

The trust we hold, a mighty shield,
To every sorrow, we shall yield,
For every step, with hope we tread,
In love's embrace, we are truly fed.

So onward, blessed, we carry forth,
Each moment rich, of endless worth,
The steps of faith, a dance divine,
In His embrace, forever shine.

In the Shadow of the Temple

Within the temple's sacred space,
We gather here, to seek His grace,
In shadows deep, the light does gleam,
A place of prayer, a holy dream.

The pillars stand, with tales to tell,
Of hearts redeemed and souls made well,
Through every stone, His spirit flows,
In quiet moments, love just grows.

With candles lit, we lift our voice,
In worship sweet, we freely rejoice,
The harmony of hearts aligned,
In the shadow, true peace we find.

Around the altar, we unite,
In shared devotion, pure delight,
The bonds of faith, unbroken, strong,
In His embrace, we all belong.

And as we leave this hallowed ground,
The pulse of faith forever bound,
In every step, His love will lead,
In the temple's shadow, we are freed.

Ribbons of Grace in Motion

In morning light we find our way,
With mercy wrapped in soft array.
The whispers of the heart's embrace,
Guide our souls through time and space.

Each step we take is laced in peace,
In every breath, our burdens cease.
A tapestry of faith unfolds,
With every thread, His love beholds.

Through trials deep and valleys low,
His hand ignites the path we sow.
In gentle prayer we rise anew,
Embracing light, our spirits grew.

Ribbons of grace, aglow, so bright,
They lead us forward, through the night.
With hope beside us, fear takes flight,
In His embrace, we find our might.

To love, to heal, to understand,
We walk together, hand in hand.
With every heartbeat, lives entwine,
In this journey, we are divine.

Divine Footprints of Love

Footprints etched upon the sand,
Remind us of a loving hand.
Each step we take, paths intertwine,
In the dance of the sacred divine.

The sun sets low, reflecting grace,
In every shadow, find His face.
He walks with us, both near and far,
Guiding light, our guiding star.

Through storms of life and quiet streams,
He holds our hearts, ignites our dreams.
In unity, all souls shall rise,
A chorus sung 'neath boundless skies.

Love's gentle hands are always there,
In whispered prayers, we find our care.
Whatever trials that we may know,
Divine footprints help us grow.

The truth prevails, forever blessed,
In love's embrace, we find our rest.
With every heartbeat, we align,
In footsteps soft, the love divine.

The Gospel of Gentle Strolls

In tranquil parks beneath the trees,
We walk with faith, with hearts at ease.
The gospel speaks in gentle tones,
In every sigh, He calls us home.

A stroll of grace, hand in hand,
In joyful moments, we understand.
The laughter shared, a sacred bond,
In quiet whispers, we respond.

As flowers bloom upon the ground,
In nature's hush, His love is found.
The path we take, though not always straight,
Is paved with hope, is filled with fate.

Through valleys deep and hills so high,
With every step, we learn to fly.
His gospel flows like streams of light,
In gentle strolls, our spirits ignite.

Let's gather strength from what we've known,
In every walk, our love has grown.
With open hearts, we hear His call,
In nature's arms, we find our all.

Embracing the Divine Tides

The waves roll in, with rhythm pure,
A dance of life, in love, secure.
Each tide that flows, a sacred trust,
In water's embrace, we rise from dust.

The ocean's breath, a hymn of grace,
Invites our hearts to find their place.
Its timeless song, a soothing balm,
In every storm, it keeps us calm.

The tides bring whispers, soft and sweet,
Where heaven's grace and earthbeats meet.
As we are washed by love's embrace,
We find our kindred, holy space.

To walk this shore, to understand,
The ebb and flow of faith's command.
With every rise, we learn to trust,
In divine tides, our hearts combust.

Embracing love, we let it guide,
Through tempest wild, He is our tide.
In harmony, our spirits soar,
With every wave, we love Him more.

Silent Prayers Beneath Our Feet

In the still of the night we kneel,
Whispers rise with every breath,
Each prayer a promise we feel,
Grounded deep beneath our steps.

Hearts unite with sacred trust,
The earth holds our silent plea,
In every pebble, every dust,
Echoes of eternity.

Mountains bow in reverence pure,
While rivers flow with grace bestowed,
We gather strength, our faith secure,
In every path that we have strode.

Nature sings in hymns of light,
The stars bear witness to our quest,
And in the shadows of the night,
We find our solace, find our rest.

So let us walk with spirits bold,
With each step, a blessing grows,
Silent prayers, a tapestry told,
Beneath our feet, divinity flows.

Breath of Heaven on Earth

In morning's glow, a whisper stirs,
Gentle winds brush against the skin,
Divine essence that softly purrs,
Breath of Heaven, let life begin.

Each flower blooms with sacred grace,
Colors dance in harmony,
We feel the warmth of love's embrace,
Nature's hymn, a symphony.

From mountains high to valleys deep,
Creation sings, resounding true,
In every heartbeat, promises keep,
The breath of Heaven, pure and new.

In twilight's shade, the spirit glows,
Crickets chirp, a lullaby,
With every breath, the silence flows,
A bond with Heaven in the sky.

So take a moment, pause, and breathe,
Let grace fill every hollow space,
In each inhale, we can believe,
Heaven's love, a warm embrace.

The Dance of Faithful Souls

In dim-lit halls where shadows play,
Faithful souls entwine and sway,
With every step, they sing in tune,
A dance of love beneath the moon.

Each heartbeat echoes sweet refrain,
A circle drawn by love's own thread,
In unity, the joy we gain,
In every doubt, through faith, we spread.

Their laughter rises, pure and bright,
In rhythm with the stars above,
Together forging in the night,
A tapestry of hope and love.

Though trials test, their spirits soar,
With hands held high, they greet the dawn,
In every challenge, hearts explore,
The dance of faith goes ever on.

So let us join this sacred waltz,
With open hearts, we find our way,
In steps of grace, we break our faults,
The dance of faith, our bright array.

Closer with Every Step

Each step we take is filled with grace,
A journey marked by light and love,
With open hearts, we seek His face,
And walk upon the path He's proved.

The road ahead may twist and turn,
Yet faith ignites our every stride,
With every lesson, hearts will burn,
In Him, our hopes and dreams abide.

Through valleys low and mountains high,
We find our strength in sacred trust,
With courage born from a silent cry,
We rise again, our hearts robust.

With every heartbeat, we draw near,
Each moment shines with purpose clear,
In love's embrace, we shed our fear,
And know, in Him, the path is dear.

So let us walk, hand in hand,
Closer with every step we take,
In unity, together we stand,
Our souls awakened for His sake.

Every Step a Testament

In faith I walk, my heart held high,
With each step forward, I touch the sky.
The path is lit by hope's pure light,
Every moment a sacred sight.

With gentle hands, I lift my prayer,
In whispers sweet, I find Him there.
The trials faced, a rugged test,
Yet through it all, my soul finds rest.

Each heartbeat echoes a truth so bold,
In every story, His grace unfolds.
With every tear and every smile,
I feel His love, transcending each mile.

As shadows fade and daylight gleams,
I walk in faith, guided by dreams.
For every stumble shall not confound,
For in His arms, my peace is found.

So onward I tread, in trust renewed,
My journey blessed, my spirit imbued.
In every step, my heart shall seek,
The love of God, forever meek.

Boundless Love on the Journey

In the dawn, I see His face,
A gentle smile, a warm embrace.
The world unfolds, a path so wide,
In every heart, He takes a ride.

With every breath, I sing His song,
In every moment, a love so strong.
Through trials faced and joys that bloom,
His boundless love dispels the gloom.

We climb the hills and cross the streams,
With faith as fuel, we chase our dreams.
In whispers soft, His call is clear,
To walk with Him, we have no fear.

Each soul we meet, a spark divine,
A glimpse of light, a holy sign.
In kindness shared, we find our way,
In unity, we rise and sway.

Together we weave this tapestry bright,
Boundless love shines, a guiding light.
With every step, our hearts do soar,
In this journey, we seek Him more.

Through the Valleys of the Spirit

In valleys low, where shadows creep,
My heart is yearning, my soul won't sleep.
Yet in the darkness, a glimmer glows,
A beacon of faith, as the Spirit flows.

With arms outstretched, I embrace the pain,
Through every struggle, a lesson gained.
The strength within, a holy fuse,
In every trial, my heart will choose.

For in the depths, His whispers call,
A promise made, I'll never fall.
Through every tear, a cleansing rain,
Rebirth awaits from every strain.

The mountains high, the valleys deep,
Through every challenge, His love I keep.
With eyes wide open, I walk the road,
Through valleys low, I bear my load.

In seeking light, I find my peace,
In every breath, my fears release.
Through valleys of spirit, I find my way,
In boundless grace, I choose to stay.

Stepping into the Divine

As dawn breaks forth, I rise in prayer,
To meet the day, my heart laid bare.
In sacred steps, I seek His face,
With every breath, I feel His grace.

To walk in light, my chosen quest,
In trusting Him, I find my rest.
The world around me, a canvas bright,
With every stroke, I share His light.

In moments still, His voice I hear,
Guiding my path, dispelling fear.
With open heart, I take each stride,
In faith and love, I walk beside.

As clouds may gather, storms may roar,
I stand unshaken, my spirit soar.
For in the tempest, He is my shield,
In every heart, His truth revealed.

So stepping forth, I know I'm free,
With every step, He walks with me.
Into the divine, I shall abide,
In every moment, my Savior, my guide.

Footfalls of Reverence

In quiet halls of grace we tread,
With humble hearts and voices fed.
Each step we take, a prayer which grows,
A whisper soft, where mercy flows.

On paths of light, our spirits rise,
Beneath the vast, embracing skies.
With every footfall, hope ignites,
In sacred realms, the soul delights.

Together bound by faith's embrace,
We seek the warmth of love's true face.
In unity, we find our song,
A melody where we belong.

As shadows flee from dawn's first glow,
We walk in peace where rivers flow.
Our reverent steps, a silent plea,
Reflecting all that's pure and free.

Thus onward still, through trials deep,
Our hearts awake, our spirits leap.
In every footfall, wisdom's call,
We strive to rise, we strive for all.

The Heart's Sacred Voyage

Upon the waves of faith we sail,
A journey woven with each tale.
Our hearts aligned with stars above,
Navigating through divine love.

With every ripple, grace unfolds,
The secrets of the heart retold.
In silence deep, where shadows part,
The compass turns—it's sacred art.

As winds of hope guide every quest,
The burdens lighten, souls find rest.
In unity, our spirits soar,
A voyage vast, forevermore.

Through tempests wild and skies serene,
We seek to glimpse the unseen sheen.
Embracing all, through tears and joy,
The heart's own call, our truest ploy.

For every wave that bends and breaks,
A deeper bond of love awakes.
Together, we chase destiny,
In sacred voyage, we are free.

Guided by Celestial Hands

In twilight's hush, we feel our way,
With faith as bright as breaking day.
Celestial hands, our touch divine,
Lead us through shadows, light we find.

Each moment crafted, every sign,
The stars align, our paths entwine.
With every heartbeat, angels near,
Their whispers soft, forever clear.

Through mountain highs and valleys low,
The grace of love will always flow.
In every trial, strength bestows,
A sacred bond as life bestows.

Together rising, hearts ablaze,
We journey forth in joyful praise.
With hands held high, in trust we stand,
All guided forth by love's great hand.

For every star that lights the night,
May we reflect that sacred light.
In harmony, our spirits sing,
Guided by all that love can bring.

Steps in the Light of Forgiveness

In gentle grace, we take our stride,
With hearts laid bare, no shame to hide.
Forgiveness blooms in fertile ground,
A healing balm, in love we're bound.

Each step we take, a bridge to mend,
To find the peace we seek, our friend.
In letting go, we find our way,
To brighter skies that greet the day.

Embracing flaws, each scar we share,
Reflects the strength of love and care.
In every choice, we're called to rise,
To lift the veil and break the ties.

As shadows pass, the light will stay,
Illuminating paths to sway.
With open hearts, we sow the seeds,
Of kindness, hope, and loving deeds.

Thus onward still, with faithful grace,
We navigate this holy space.
In steps of light, our souls unite,
Forgiveness shines, a sacred light.

Whispered Prayers Along the Way

In shadows deep, I bow my head,
With whispered prayers, my soul is fed.
Each moment spent, in grace I dwell,
The heart's true yearn, my spirit's swell.

Beneath the stars, I find my peace,
In silent night, my fears release.
With gentle faith, I walk the land,
A guiding light, a steady hand.

Through trials faced, I find my path,
In love's warm light, I escape wrath.
The sacred truth, a beacon bright,
Illuminates the darkest night.

With every step, I seek to grow,
In holy whispers, my spirit flows.
The journey long, yet sweet and pure,
In faith's embrace, my heart's secure.

So onward now, my prayers ascend,
Through valleys low, my soul I send.
In every breath, a sacred song,
With whispered prayers, I will belong.

The Horizon of Belief

Beyond the hills, the sun will rise,
A promise new beneath the skies.
With each new dawn, the heart will sing,
Of faith's embrace, a holy thing.

The horizon glows with hope's bright flame,
In whispered dreams, I call His name.
Each step I take, a journey true,
In love's warm light, I start anew.

With open arms, I greet the day,
In every choice, I find my way.
Beneath the clouds, I feel Him near,
In every joy, and every tear.

The winds of change, they softly blow,
In faith's embrace, my spirit grows.
As shadows fade, my heart takes flight,
Upon the horizon, purest light.

So here I stand, with faith my guide,
In every prayer, I do abide.
With open heart, I rise above,
In all my days, I feel His love.

Rising with Each Sacred Step

With every footfall, grace is found,
In sacred spaces, I am bound.
I rise anew with hopes so bright,
In trust's embrace, I feel the light.

The mountains high, they call my name,
In every echo, love's sweet flame.
I tread the path, both rough and clear,
Each step a prayer, each breath sincere.

In valleys low, my spirit soars,
As faith restores what hope implores.
The journey long, yet rich and real,
With every trial, a chance to heal.

With sacred songs, I walk the way,
In all my heart, His words will stay.
Through winds that shift, and storms that come,
In every beat, my spirit hums.

So here I stand, my soul in flight,
With each new dawn, I find the light.
In every step, in every breath,
I rise with love, defying death.

A Journey Through the Holy Valley

Through hills adorned, the valley flows,
In sacred whispers, truth bestows.
With every turn, a lesson learned,
In faith's embrace, my heart is turned.

The rivers run, with purpose clear,
In every drop, the love draws near.
With grace I walk, through trials faced,
In holy light, my fears erased.

Among the trees, I feel Him breathe,
In every leaf, my soul believes.
Through paths of stone, and fields of gold,
A sacred journey to behold.

With every prayer, the spirits rise,
In humble trust, I claim the skies.
The holy valley calls my name,
In every step, I seek the same.

So let me walk, in peace abide,
Through holy lands, with love as guide.
With every heartbeat, pure and true,
A journey blessed, for me and you.

Harmonies of Hopeful Steps

In quiet dawn the angels sing,
A melody of love takes wing.
Each step we take, a prayer in flight,
Guided by faith, embracing light.

Through valleys deep and mountains high,
We weave our dreams beneath the sky.
With hands held close, we rise anew,
Bound by the trust in love so true.

The road is long, yet we are strong,
In unity, we hum along.
Our hearts aligned, a sacred song,
Together we belong, we belong.

When shadows fall, we seek the flame,
In every heart, his love we claim.
With hopeful steps, we bravely tread,
For every word our Savior said.

So let us walk through trials faced,
In every tear, His warmth embraced.
With harmonies that gently guide,
We share His peace, forever bide.

The Covenant of Caring Journeys

We travel paths of sacred trust,
In each encounter, love is just.
Through laughter shared and sorrows worn,
A covenant of hearts is borne.

With every mile, our spirits blend,
On journeys steep, we find a friend.
In acts of grace, we pave the way,
For kindness blooms in bright array.

The burdens shared, the joy we weave,
A tapestry of hearts that cleave.
In moments small, our light shines bright,
Each step reflects His purest light.

Through storms that rage, we stand as one,
In shadows cast, our hope still runs.
With open hands, we share our song,
In caring ways, we all belong.

As we embark on paths unknown,
United by the love we've grown.
The covenant we cherish dear,
In every step, God's love is near.

Traces of the Beloved's Path

Along the trails where footsteps fade,
The Beloved's grace is gently laid.
In whispers soft, His words we hear,
Guiding our hearts, banishing fear.

With every breath, His love we trace,
In nature's embrace, we find our place.
In fragrant blooms and rivers wide,
The echoes of His heart confide.

Through trials faced and love reborn,
In shadows cast, our souls are worn.
We find the strength to rise above,
In every moment, we seek His love.

A shared journey, a sacred bond,
In unity, we dream beyond.
With hands entwined, in trust we roam,
The Beloved leads us safely home.

In every step, His footprints glow,
And in each heart, a flame to grow.
As traces of His path we find,
We walk together, intertwined.

A Sojourn of Seraphic Love

In tender hues of dawn's embrace,
We venture forth in sacred space.
With seraphic grace, our spirits soar,
In love's embrace, we seek for more.

With every heartbeat, trust unfolds,
In every story, love retold.
Through trials faced and joys we share,
A sojourn blessed, with hearts laid bare.

Beneath the stars, our hopes align,
In every prayer, His light will shine.
With wings of faith, we rise and sing,
Eternal bonds that love will bring.

Through valleys deep, to mountains wide,
In seraph's arms, we learn to glide.
With every challenge, new heights soar,
In love's embrace, we find our core.

So let us dance through night and day,
In seraphic love, we'll find our way.
For every step, a promise made,
Together, love will never fade.

The Language of Graceful Movement

In whispered winds, we find our way,
Each step a prayer, as night turns to day.
Hearts in sync with the softest breeze,
A dance of souls among the trees.

With every turn, a sacred call,
In unity, we stand or fall.
The rhythm of life, a gentle song,
In faith we move, where we belong.

Hands outstretched, we reach for light,
Navigating shadows, embracing night.
In silent grace, the spirit guides,
Within our hearts, the truth abides.

Through valleys deep, on mountains high,
The language of grace will never die.
With open hearts, we tread the earth,
In every step, we find new birth.

So let us walk this path divine,
With trust in Him, our hearts align.
In graceful movement, we find our peace,
In every step, His love will cease.

Streams of Faithful Exploration

In tranquil waters, we seek the dawn,
Where faith flows freely, never withdrawn.
Ripples of grace, in whispers tell,
The sacred stories, the tales that swell.

Guided by light, we sail along,
In every wave, the spirit's song.
Each splash a moment, a gift of trust,
With every current, our hearts adjust.

Through valleys wide and mountains steep,
In streams of faith, our souls shall leap.
The journey long, yet never vain,
In exploration, joy and pain.

In quiet pools, reflections grow,
Mirrors of grace, where wisdom flows.
We search for truth in every glance,
In faith's embrace, we learn to dance.

So let the waters flow and guide,
In every stream, the Lord provides.
Faithful hearts, together we roam,
In streams of love, we find our home.

Threads of Serenity in the Pilgrim's Way

In the fabric of life, we weave our trust,
With threads of hope, our dreams adjust.
Each stitch a moment, a prayer intense,
In the tapestry's flow, we find recompense.

On pilgrim paths, where shadows fall,
The steps we take, a silent call.
Through challenges faced and joys embraced,
In every journey, His love is traced.

With gentle hands, we spin the yarn,
In every struggle, we find the dawn.
As threads entwine, our spirits rise,
In serenity's arms, our hearts harmonize.

Through winding roads, both steep and mild,
In faith's embrace, we are like a child.
We gather strength from every thread,
In the fabric of grace, our fears are shed.

So may we walk this pilgrim's way,
In woven trust, we shall not sway.
With threads of serenity, we are bound,
In love's design, our hope is found.

Pathways of Devotion

In pathways wide, where footsteps meet,
We walk in faith, our hearts in beat.
With every choice, a sacred vow,
In devotion's light, we find our now.

Beneath the stars, our spirits soar,
In whispered prayers, we seek for more.
The road ahead, a promise true,
Guided by love in all we do.

Through trials faced, and moments shared,
In faith's embrace, we are prepared.
Each step a testament to grace,
On devotion's path, we find our place.

With open hearts, we share the load,
In unity of spirit, we walk the road.
Compassionate whispers, the guiding light,
In every turn, we spread our might.

So let us journey with hearts aligned,
In pathways of devotion, we are defined.
In steadfast love, our lives shall glow,
With every step, His kindness we sow.

The Road Less Traveled with Grace

In whispers soft, the path unfolds,
A journey blessed, where faith beholds.
With every step, the heart will soar,
Embraced by love, we seek the door.

The winding road beneath our feet,
Where trials meet, and angels greet.
With hands held high, we walk in light,
For grace will guide us through the night.

In shadows deep, our spirits rise,
The heavens gleam in soulful skies.
Through valleys low and peaks so grand,
We walk together, hand in hand.

A tapestry of hope we weave,
Each thread a prayer, each breath we cleave.
In every turn, a lesson found,
With grace, we dance on holy ground.

So let us roam where few have tread,
With faith as light, and heart as lead.
The road less traveled, bright and wide,
With grace, our ever-present guide.

Pilgrimage of the Soul

In quiet moments, the soul takes flight,
A sacred journey, day and night.
Through mountains high and valleys deep,
We seek the truth, and gently weep.

Each footstep marks a prayer profound,
In every silence, love is found.
With open hearts, we share our dreams,
The path illuminated by love's beams.

Through trials faced, our spirits grow,
With faith as compass, we come to know.
Each sacred pause a chance to breathe,
In pilgrimage, our souls believe.

Together we weave a tapestry,
Of trials faced, and joyful glee.
In every heart, a sacred beat,
As pilgrims walk on hallowed street.

With every dawn, new hope is born,
Together, we rise, no longer torn.
The pilgrimage, a divine embrace,
In each of us, the holy grace.

Strides of Serenity

In tranquil dawn, the spirit wakes,
With every breath, our soul partakes.
Through fields of green, we walk with ease,
In nature's arms, we find our peace.

Each step we take, a mindful prayer,
In every moment, love to share.
With hearts aligned, we hear the call,
To cherish life, embrace it all.

The rivers flow, like grace anew,
In silence found, our hearts break through.
As sunlight dances on the floor,
We find our calm, forevermore.

Through whispered trees, the spirit sings,
In harmony, the hope it brings.
With gentle strides, we seek the light,
Serenity our guiding sight.

So let us wander, hand in hand,
In this blessed, holy land.
With every footfall, peace extends,
In strides of grace, our journey blends.

The Sacred Silence in Our Steps

In sacred silence, hearts unite,
With every step, we seek the light.
Through gentle paths, our spirits roam,
In whispered grace, we find our home.

The echoes of our dreams resound,
In quiet faith, our hopes are found.
With mindful breath, we walk in tune,
Beneath the stars, beneath the moon.

Each pause invites the soul to see,
The beauty forged in harmony.
The stillness deep, a sacred song,
In silence strong, we all belong.

Through trials faced, our hearts remain,
In sacred silence, joy and pain.
Every journey fraught with grace,
A holy space we all embrace.

So let us tread where few have gone,
With spirits bright, we carry on.
In every step, the love we keep,
In sacred silence, our souls leap.

Soulful Wanderings on Celestial Roads

In the silence I seek the light,
Whispers of the stars in the night.
Each step I take is a prayer,
Guided by faith, free from despair.

The moon helps me find my way,
Illuminating paths where shadows play.
I wander deep through the holy mist,
Every moment a sacred tryst.

Embracing truth in every breath,
In the dance of life and death.
With each heartbeat, I learn to feel,
The warmth of grace, a soothing seal.

Together we rise beyond the veil,
On celestial roads, our spirits sail.
Surrendered souls, we seek and find,
Unity woven in the divine.

So onward along these paths we roam,
With each soft step, we carve a home.
In the sacred fields of love's embrace,
We walk forever in quiet grace.

The Sanctity of Each Step

With humble heart, I tread the ground,
In every footfall, blessings found.
The earth beneath, so full of life,
Each moment precious, free from strife.

In the stillness, I hear the call,
A whisper guiding one and all.
Each step a testament of faith,
In the journey's embrace, I find my place.

The light within begins to glow,
A radiant truth; it's all I know.
Around me, nature's hymn does swell,
In every note, a tale to tell.

Prayer rises with every motion,
In sacred rhythm, I find devotion.
With spirit bright and heart aligned,
The sanctity of steps entwined.

I walk in love, the world so vast,
Each breath a moment meant to last.
Boundless horizons call my name,
In the sacred dance, I'll play my game.

Righteous Pathways Under Starlit Skies

Underneath a sky adorned with dreams,
Guided by light, or so it seems.
My footsteps trace the ancient lines,
Where wisdom echoes, softly shines.

The stars above, like scattered jewels,
Remind us of the cosmic rules.
Each path I walk is meant to be,
A journey deep, the soul set free.

In the stillness, I find my guide,
With faith, I open wide my stride.
The moonlight paints the way ahead,
Each step a prayer, each word unsaid.

Righteous pathways stretch and bend,
In every curve, I find a friend.
With open heart, I seek the truth,
In simple grace, I reclaim my youth.

Together we walk through night and day,
Finding peace along the way.
With starlit skies to light our fears,
We dance through life, embracing years.

Illuminated by Grace

In the dawn where shadows flee,
I find my path, where I am free.
The sun arises in gentle embrace,
Illuminated by divine grace.

Every heartbeat tells the tale,
Of sacred love that will not fail.
With each soft breeze, I feel the call,
In grace, I rise, I will not fall.

Colors burst in morning light,
Nature sings in pure delight.
I walk in faith through open gates,
In harmony with all that waits.

The blessings rain from heavens high,
As hopes and dreams begin to fly.
With gratitude, my spirit soars,
In love's embrace, forevermore.

In this journey, hand in hand,
We spread compassion through the land.
United in grace, we carry on,
With every step, a sacred song.

Treading the Aisles of Mercy

In the gentle light of dawn, we walk,
With humble hearts, we whisper and talk.
Each step we take, a prayer in the air,
Finding solace, knowing You are there.

Through aisles of mercy, we seek Your face,
Embracing love, wrapped in Your grace.
For every soul, a story unfolds,
In the warmth of compassion, our hearts behold.

With outstretched hands, we gather near,
Sharing our burdens, lifting our fear.
In unity, we tread this sacred ground,
A community of grace, where hope is found.

O gentle Shepherd, guide our way,
In the quiet moments, let us pray.
With faith, we journey, hand in hand,
In the aisles of mercy, we make our stand.

As the sun sets, we pause to reflect,
In Your embrace, our hearts connect.
Treading softly on this holy path,
With love as our compass, we find our worth.

The Sacred Journey of the Giving Heart

In every heartbeat lies a sacred tale,
Of love that flourishes, never to pale.
With open hands, our gifts we share,
A journey of giving, a heartfelt prayer.

Through trials faced, we find our way,
In kindness given, we choose to stay.
The giving heart knows no bounds,
In the depths of love, true joy resounds.

Each moment shared, a treasure to keep,
In the light of grace, our souls take a leap.
For every act of kindness we show,
The seeds of faith in our hearts will grow.

With every step, we learn and grow,
The road of giving, a sacred flow.
In the laughter shared, and tears we shed,
The journey unfolds, where angels tread.

And when our time here comes to an end,
In the legacy of love, we transcend.
For the sacred journey is never in vain,
In the giving heart, we forever remain.

Vinculum of Graceful Endeavors

In every heart lies a graceful thread,
Connecting our souls to the path we tread.
With kindness woven through each endeavor,
A vinculum strong, binding us forever.

Through trials and triumphs, we rise and fall,
In unity's strength, we heed the call.
Each step in faith, a dance divine,
In the light of truth, our spirits align.

With every word of comfort we give,
We nurture the bond in which we live.
In laughter and sorrow, we stand as one,
The grace in our hearts, a radiant sun.

As rivers of hope flow into the sea,
We embrace each other, in strong decree.
Woven together, through love's sweet grace,
In this sacred dance, we find our place.

For every endeavor that we partake,
The vinculum of grace, we'll never break.
In the hands of love, our dreams take flight,
Forever united, through day and night.

Stories Woven in the Tread of Time

In the fabric of life, our stories reside,
Woven with threads of love, side by side.
Each moment a stitch, from joy to strife,
In the tapestry of faith, we find our life.

Through trials endured and victories won,
In the light of hope, our hearts are spun.
With every whisper of the winds that blow,
The stories we tell of the love we know.

Every soul a tale, uniquely designed,
In the book of life, our hearts intertwined.
From laughter shared to tears we shed,
In the stories woven, love's journey is spread.

As the stars unveil their shimmering light,
We gather our truths, embracing the night.
With the wisdom of ages, we humbly learn,
In the tread of time, our spirits yearn.

For each chapter penned is a gift we share,
In the stories of life, we find our prayer.
In unity's embrace, let our hearts chime,
For we are the authors in the tread of time.

The Rise of Compassionate Hearts

In shadows deep where kindness hides,
A gentle light within abides.
Compassion blooms in every tear,
Its whispers echo, drawing near.

The weary souls, they lift their gaze,
In gratitude, they sing His praise.
For every heart that dares to care,
Brings forth a hope, beyond despair.

Through trials faced and burdens shared,
In acts of love, we find we're paired.
Together, weaving threads of grace,
In unity, we find our place.

With open arms, we greet the day,
Our hearts aligned in pure array.
For mercy flows like rivers wide,
Embracing all, with arms open wide.

So let compassion rise and soar,
In every life, let kindness pour.
As hearts awake and spirits start,
We usher in a brand new part.

Walking Through the Valley of Blessings

In valleys low where shadows creep,
We walk with faith, our promise deep.
With every step, a prayer we share,
Guided by grace, we need not fear.

The blessings bloom like flowers bright,
Illuminating darkest night.
In trials faced, His hand we feel,
A shepherd's love, our wounds to heal.

Through gentle streams and mountains tall,
He whispers hope to one and all.
With every turn, His presence near,
In every breath, we cast out fear.

In unity, our spirits thrive,
As blessings flow, we come alive.
Together held in heavenly light,
We journey forth, embracing night.

So let us walk with hearts of song,
In valleys where we all belong.
For every trial, a lesson learned,
In gratitude, our hearts returned.

Footprint of the Faithful Divine

In sand and stone, His footprints trace,
A map of love, our sacred space.
With every stride, His light we seek,
In silent prayers, our souls shall speak.

The faithful walk where shadows loom,
Their faith ignites like flowers bloom.
In storms of doubt and trials steep,
They find their strength in love so deep.

Through every joy and every pain,
The footprints guide us once again.
In moments still, we pause to see,
The path of light that sets us free.

With open hearts, we follow through,
The whispers sacred, ever true.
In unity, we boldly tread,
On paths of light where angels led.

So mark the ground with love and care,
For every step, He is right there.
In reverence, we honor divine,
The journey blessed, His love enshrined.

Walks of Joy in Solitude's Embrace

In quiet woods where silence dwells,
We find the peace that gently swells.
In solitude, our hearts take flight,
A sacred dance in morning light.

With every breath, the world we greet,
In gentle whispers, hope so sweet.
The joy of stillness fills the air,
In every moment, love we share.

As nature's hymn begins to play,
We walk with joy, come what may.
In solitude, our spirits rise,
Reflecting truth in clear blue skies.

With every step, the heart expands,
In tender grace, it understands.
The gift of time, a treasured space,
In solitude, we find His grace.

So let us walk where peace invites,
With open hearts, in pure delights.
For in this stillness, we embrace,
The joy of love, in every place.

Steps Toward Celestial Peace

In silence, we seek the light,
Paths of grace, shining bright.
With every prayer, hearts align,
Finding solace, so divine.

In surrender, burdens cease,
Trusting love, we find our peace.
Whispers soft, the spirit guides,
Through the storms, the faith abides.

Hope like stars in darkest night,
Glimmers soft, a wondrous sight.
Each step forward, spirits soar,
In unity, we seek for more.

With hearts open, we embrace,
Grace flows freely, warm and trace.
Every moment, acts so pure,
In kindness, our souls mature.

Together in this sacred space,
Treasured paths we now retrace.
With loving hands, we serve each day,
Steps toward peace, our hearts will sway.

The Dance of Devotion's Voyage

In the rhythm of the heart,
Life's ballet, it plays a part.
With every prayer, feet align,
In devotion, love will shine.

Through trials, we sway and spin,
Finding strength that lies within.
In harmony, our voices rise,
Whispers echo, reaching skies.

With each movement, souls ignite,
Dancing through the endless night.
In the stillness, light unfolds,
Stories of the brave and bold.

The world fades, but love will stay,
Guiding us upon our way.
In the steps that we embrace,
Life's a dance, a sacred space.

Let us gather, hand in hand,
In devotion, we will stand.
With hearts ablaze, we'll voyage free,
In this dance, we'll find the key.

Sowing Seeds of Kindness Along the Way

In the soil of compassion, we sow,
Each little act, a radiant glow.
With open hearts, we break the ground,
In small gestures, love is found.

Nurturing hopes like flowers bloom,
In each seed, dispelling gloom.
The warmth of kindness spreads afar,
Guided gently by a star.

Through laughter shared and tears embraced,
Compassion's quilt, a warm encased.
With every word, we lift, we mend,
In simple acts, we find a friend.

As we walk this sacred trail,
Each step taken will prevail.
In kindness spread, our spirits soar,
A legacy of love, we pour.

Let's sow the seeds, let's tend the land,
As one community, hand in hand.
For in this journey, joy will stay,
Together strong, we'll find our way.

In the Footsteps of the Faithful

Walking paths of those before,
In their footprints, we explore.
Every step a story shared,
In their courage, hearts are bared.

From the mountains to the seas,
Their wisdom carries like the breeze.
With each word of love they spoke,
Our spirits rise, no more revoked.

In their shadows, we find our light,
Through the darkness, we ignite.
Trail of hope, we now pursue,
In their grace, we blossom too.

With every prayer, we walk as one,
In the dawn of a brand new sun.
Across the ages, faith endures,
In gentle hands, love reassures.

Together, we'll follow their lead,
In their footsteps, we plant the seed.
With steadfast hearts, we will repay,
In the faith of the faithful, we stay.

Each Step a Prayer

Each step I take in silent grace,
A whisper of faith in this sacred place.
With every breath, my spirit sings,
In the rhythm of life, my heart takes wings.

The burdens I carry, laid at His feet,
In this humble act, my soul feels complete.
Through trials and joys, I find my way,
Each step a prayer, come what may.

In the still of the night, I seek His face,
In solitude, I enter His embrace.
With hands lifted high, I pour out my heart,
A sacred connection, never to part.

Through valleys low and mountains steep,
His presence surrounds, my spirit to keep.
With faith as my guide, in shadows I tread,
Each step a prayer, where angels have led.

In the dawn of each day, with hope I rise,
Gazing up high, where my spirit flies.
With every heartbeat, I'm blessed to say,
Each step a prayer, come what may.

The Journey of Devotion's Hand

Upon this path where shadows blend,
I walk in faith, my spirit to mend.
With every trial, strength I gain,
In the silence, I hear His reign.

From dawn's first light to twilight's glow,
Each moment a blessing, a seed I sow.
In gratitude's arms, I find my peace,
The journey unfolds, my spirit's lease.

His guiding hand, a gentle touch,
In every corner, I feel His clutch.
With open heart, I dare to dream,
In devotion's flow, I find my theme.

Through every storm, His love will stay,
A compass of hope that lights my way.
Each heartbeat echoes His divine plan,
In every step, I hold His hand.

At journey's end, I'll look back and see,
The grace that's walked alongside of me.
With joy I'll sing of love's sweet strand,
In the journey of devotion's hand.

Blessings on the Path of Love

In the garden of grace, I plant my seeds,
With every thought, I sow the deeds.
In kindness and light, my heart shall dwell,
Upon this path, where blessings swell.

Each step I take, a love reborn,
In the sunlight's glow, the day is worn.
With open arms, I receive the morn,
Blessings abound, a new day is sworn.

Through laughter shared and tears that flow,
In love's embrace, our spirits grow.
With every touch, I'm reminded of grace,
The warmth of His love, a soft embrace.

As rivers run deep and mountains rise high,
The blessings weave where hearts comply.
On this path of love, I'll always be,
A vessel of light, eternally free.

In twilight's glow, I reflect on the day,
Each moment a gift, in love's sweet play.
With gratitude flowing, my heart's in tow,
Blessings on this path of love I know.

Navigating by Heavenly Stars

Beneath the night sky, I drift and dream,
Guided by stars, in a gentle beam.
Each twinkle a whisper, a truth revealed,
In the cosmos' embrace, my heart is healed.

With faith as my sailor, I chart the way,
Through darkened waters, where shadows lay.
In celestial light, my soul takes flight,
Navigating by stars, a beacon bright.

When storms arise and doubts collide,
I raise my gaze, and in Him confide.
His love's the anchor, steadfast and true,
In the dance of the heavens, I'm drawn anew.

With every dawn that breaks the night,
A canvas of hope, painted with light.
In the vast expanse, I'm never alone,
Navigating by stars, I find my home.

So here I wander, in peace I roam,
With faith my compass, and love my home.
In the tapestry of night, my heart's desire,
Navigating by heavenly stars, I aspire.

Walking in the Light of Compassion

In the stillness, love unfolds,
A beacon bright, warm and bold.
With every step, a heart aligned,
Together we find, compassion defined.

Through shadows cast, we gently tread,
With kindred spirits, our paths are led.
Hands held high, our souls ignite,
In the journey pure, we walk in light.

Each whisper shared, a prayer in time,
We lift the fallen, our voices rhyme.
With open hearts, we pave the way,
In love's embrace, forever stay.

The world around, in need we see,
As kindness blooms, we set it free.
In every tear, a lesson learned,
For in love's fire, our spirits burned.

The call is simple, yet profound,
With each small act, new hope is found.
We rise as one, hearts intertwined,
In the tapestry of grace, we're blind.

Together we walk, hand in hand,
In the light of love, we strongly stand.
With every heart, and every dream,
In compassion's glow, we brightly gleam.

Sacred Soles and Silent Prayers

As I tread on sacred ground,
With every step, my soul is found.
In silent prayers, I seek the way,
With faith as light, I choose to stay.

Beneath the sky, my spirit soars,
In whispered winds, my heart adores.
With soles that dance on paths divine,
I feel the presence, forever shine.

Each journey shared, a bond profound,
In sacred moments, truth is found.
With every heartbeat, grace unfolds,
In silent prayers, a story told.

In nature's arms, I find the peace,
A gentle love that will not cease.
With every breath, my heart complies,
In sacred soles, where mercy lies.

Through trials faced, we come alive,
In silent prayers, our hopes arrive.
With faith renewed, we walk as one,
Underneath the endless sun.

The Mosaic of Graceful Strides

In every step, a story we weave,
A tapestry of love, we believe.
With graceful strides, the world unfolds,
In every heart, a truth that holds.

Together we dance on sacred paths,
In unity's song, the heart it casts.
With every heartbeat, we share the grace,
In the mosaic of life, we find our place.

Each stumble met, in love's embrace,
We rise anew, with courage and grace.
In the gentle light, our spirits soar,
As we walk together, forevermore.

In the quiet moments, wisdom flows,
Like rivers of mercy, love ever grows.
With each connection, we bridge the divide,
In the mosaic of life, our hearts reside.

Through trials faced, we learn to see,
The beauty found in harmony.
With every stride, the journey sings,
In love's embrace, our spirit springs.

With arms wide open, we greet the dawn,
In graceful strides, we carry on.
With joyous hearts, together we rise,
In the mosaic of love, we touch the skies.

In the Shadow of His Embrace

In the shadow, love's gentle sigh,
With every heartbeat, we draw nigh.
In His embrace, the world unwinds,
With open hearts, true peace we find.

As whispers linger, grace descends,
In sacred moments, the spirit mends.
With every tear, a lesson shines,
In the shadow, His love aligns.

Through valleys deep, our faith remains,
In His embrace, we bear no chains.
With light that guides, our souls combine,
In the shadow of love, we're truly fine.

In gentle breezes, we hear the call,
Uniting souls, breaking down the wall.
With every step, His promise stays,
In His embrace, we sing His praise.

In the quiet night, where hope abides,
In the shadow, the heart confides.
With every breath, we hold the grace,
In the shadow of Him, we find our place.

Together we walk, through thick and thin,
In the shadow of His love, we win.
With joyful hearts, we rise above,
In His embrace, we share the love.

Spirit-Led Journeys of the Heart

In silence, whispers of truth arise,
Guiding steps beneath the vast skies.
With faith as a lantern, bright and warm,
Each heartbeat calls, a divine charm.

The pathway winds through valleys of grace,
With each encounter, we find our place.
Hands uplifted, hearts open wide,
In sacred moments, we abide.

The spirit leads through shadows and light,
Transforming questions into pure insight.
In trials faced, the lessons bloom,
With every step, joy dispels the gloom.

We walk in rhythm, a holy dance,
Unified by purpose, given a chance.
Eternal echoes through the sacred night,
In love's embrace, we find our sight.

With every journey, a story unfolds,
In faith's embrace, true courage holds.
For in the heart where spirit ignites,
Divine paths guide through darkest nights.

Crossroads of the Soulful Walk

At the crossroads where choices align,
The soul seeks wisdom, profoundly divine.
Each path diverges, a story calls,
In holy guidance, our spirit sprawls.

Quiet moments in the morning hush,
Clarity found in the gentle rush.
Though doubts may linger, truth speaks clear,
In the heart's journey, we conquer fear.

With every step, the spirit shines bright,
A lantern of hope in the dimmest night.
At each intersection, surrender and pray,
For love's wise whispers will show the way.

Embracing change in the ebb and flow,
The sacred dance of the spirit's glow.
With trust in this journey, we fully engage,
In the rhythm of life, wisdom's page.

So choose with courage, let love prevail,
For guidance lies in the heart's holy trail.
In every crossroads, remember the call,
To walk in grace, and rise after the fall.

In the Embrace of Holy Currents

In the embrace of rivers divine,
We float on waves, sacred and fine.
The current flows, gentle yet strong,
Carrying whispers, the universe's song.

Each ripple tells of a journey made,
Through valleys of sorrow and sunlight's blade.
In the depths of the pool, secrets reside,
Guiding our hearts along the tide.

The holy currents, they twist and turn,
In their embrace, for truth, we yearn.
We trust the flow, let go of control,
For love's great wisdom awakens the soul.

With open hearts, we dance on the shore,
Finding our purpose as we explore.
In the waters of grace, we dip and dive,
In sacred depths, our spirits thrive.

So let us journey in this holy stream,
With faith as our anchor, our hearts agleam.
In every twist, and every rise,
We find connection beyond the skies.

The Rhythm of Redeeming Strolls

In the rhythm of strolls that redeem,
We walk hand in hand, sharing a dream.
With every step, a promise is made,
In love's warm glow, all fears fade.

The path is marked with blessings untold,
Each moment cherished, a treasure of gold.
As we journey together, side by side,
In faith's embrace, we shall abide.

We dance through trials, rejoice in grace,
Finding the beauty in each sacred place.
With hearts open wide, we witness the truth,
In the rhythm of life, we preserve our youth.

Through hills and valleys, our spirits align,
Connected by love, the sacred design.
In the laughter shared, in the tears we shed,
The rhythm of redeeming, a path we tread.

So let us stroll through the world with ease,
In the dance of life, our spirits tease.
With every heartbeat, our souls take flight,
In the rhythm of love, we shine bright.

In the Stillness of Every Step

In the quiet path we tread,
Whispers of grace softly spread.
Each moment holds a sacred light,
Guiding souls through day and night.

Faith unfolds like petals bright,
Kissed by dawn's gentle sight.
Step by step, we seek the divine,
In the stillness, hearts entwine.

Clarity blooms in the silence profound,
In each heartbeat, love is found.
With every breath, a hymn resounds,
In the stillness, true peace abounds.

Trust the journey, embrace the flow,
In each footfall, blessings grow.
Heaven's whispers, soft and clear,
In the stillness, we draw near.

Hold the sacred in every glance,
Life's a prayer, a holy dance.
In the stillness, find the way,
In every step, we learn to say.

Rhapsody in Prayer

In the hush of evening's glow,
Voices rise, harmonies slow.
Each prayer a note, sweet and pure,
A rhapsody, our hearts allure.

Hands lifted high, we reach for grace,
In every plea, we find our place.
A chorus of souls, united as one,
In rapture of prayer, our spirits run.

The echo of faith, a soft refrain,
In sacred silence, we remain.
With each whispered word, we ascend,
In the rhapsody, our souls mend.

Trust the rhythm, let it flow,
In every note, our spirits grow.
Seek the light in all we share,
Together we weave this rhapsody of prayer.

In the stillness, the heart's melody sings,
Embracing the love that each moment brings.
Rhapsody in prayer, a timeless embrace,
In unity, we find grace.

Navigating the Sacred Terrain

On this path of the sacred quest,
We journey forth, seeking the blessed.
With hearts like compasses, ever aware,
Guided by light, we wander and dare.

Through valleys low and mountains high,
In nature's embrace, our spirits fly.
Every step, a divine embrace,
Navigating through time and space.

The sacred terrain, a wreath of stars,
Reminds us of the love that's ours.
With faith as our map, we forge ahead,
On this journey, our hearts are fed.

Embrace the shadows, welcome the sun,
In the sacred, we are all one.
Through every trial, we rise and grow,
Navigating where grace will flow.

Hand in hand through sacred lands,
Together we stand, united we'll expand.
Trust the journey, and feel the sway,
In the sacred terrain, forever stay.

The Promise of Each Footfall

In the promise of every footfall,
We find our way, in love we call.
The earth beneath, a sacred ground,
In every step, the lost are found.

With faith we tread on paths unseen,
In the silence, the spirit's glean.
Each footfall whispers of hope anew,
The promise of grace, forever true.

As the river flows, so does our heart,
In unity, we play our part.
With every stride, we leave behind,
The chains of doubt, the heart refined.

Trust the journey, embrace the now,
In the promise, make the vow.
For in each footfall, life unfolds,
The promise of love, eternally holds.

In this journey of sacred sighs,
Each footfall echoes where the spirit flies.
Together we walk, hand in hand,
The promise of peace in this land.

Pilgrimage of Peaceful Intent

In quiet woods, our spirits soar,
With hearts aflame, we seek and explore.
Each step we take, a prayer in the air,
To find the peace that lingers there.

Through valleys low, and mountains wide,
We walk in faith, with love as our guide.
Every breath, a song of grace,
A sacred dance in this holy place.

Beneath the sky, where shadows fade,
The light of truth will never evade.
With open hearts, we share our creed,
In unity, we plant the seed.

In moments still, we pause to sigh,
Reflecting on the how and why.
Together bound, in joy we stand,
A journey blessed by a guiding hand.

So onward now, we face the morn,
With gentle hope, our hearts reborn.
In every step, love's bounty shared,
A pilgrimage where souls are bared.

Steps of a Loving Pilgrim

With gentle grace, the footsteps fall,
In silent prayer, we heed the call.
Through trials faced, our spirits shine,
In love's embrace, the souls entwine.

A loving heart, the truest guide,
In every tear, we find the tide.
Through valleys deep, and skies so bright,
Compassion's pulse, our beacon light.

With every dawn, fresh hopes arise,
In unity, we share the skies.
From mountain peaks to river bends,
Our journey flows, as love transcends.

In every smile, a prayer is sown,
Through kindness shared, we've truly grown.
Together we walk, hand in hand,
A timeless bond in this sacred land.

So let us tread on paths of peace,
In loving pilgrimage, may strife cease.
With hearts ablaze, we forge ahead,
In every step, by spirit led.

The Stones of Piety's Path

Each stone we tread, a tale untold,
Of faith and hope, in hearts so bold.
In sacred trust, we lift our gaze,
To honor those who've worn this maze.

With feet that ache, we press along,
In worship's song, we grow more strong.
The gravel whispers stories past,
While prayers ascend, our shadows cast.

Through every trial, the path we weave,
A testament of those who believe.
On every stone, their dreams reside,
In piety's light, our hearts abide.

So hand in hand, we walk with grace,
In reverence, we trace this space.
Each step reflects a sacred trust,
In love's embrace, our hearts adjust.

In the stillness, we find our way,
Through twilight's glow and break of day.
With pure intent, the stones align,
In piety's path, our souls entwine.

The Light Leading Our Journey

In darkest night, a beacon gleams,
A guiding star, where hope redeems.
With arms outstretched, we walk the line,
Embracing light, divine design.

Through shadowed lanes, our spirits glide,
In faith and love, we shall abide.
Each step we take, the light prevails,
Illuminating ancient trails.

As dawn breaks forth, the path is clear,
With hearts aglow, we draw nigh here.
In every breath, the light ignites,
A promise kept in sacred heights.

Through valleys deep, where shadows creep,
We journey on, our blessings keep.
Together bound, in light's embrace,
In love's reflection, we find our place.

So let us walk with spirits high,
In every heartbeat, the light draws nigh.
With faithful steps, our path we choose,
In love's great light, we cannot lose.

In the Footprints of the Believers

In the quiet whispers, faith does speak,
Guiding the hearts that feel so weak.
With every step, they find the way,
In the footprints of believers, they pray.

Through storms of doubt, their spirits soar,
In the love of the Lord, they find their core.
Sharing grace in every breath,
United in truth, conquering death.

Each voice a beacon, shining bright,
Proclaiming hope, a sacred light.
Their hands uplift the weary soul,
In the warmth of kindness, they are whole.

They walk together on this path,
Filled with compassion and joy that lasts.
In the darkest nights, they hold their kin,
In the footprints of believers, love shall win.

With every sorrow, every tear,
They find strength in prayer, drawing near.
A circle of faith that never ends,
Through the footprints of believers, grace transcends.

A Venture to the Radiant Light

In the dawn of promise, we take our flight,
A venture unfolds toward radiant light.
Guided by stars that shimmer and gleam,
In the heart of faith, we dare to dream.

With each step forward, burdens we shed,
Trusting the path where angels tread.
In the arms of the Divine, we find our peace,
A venture to light, where fears release.

Echoes of wisdom in the rustling leaves,
Nature whispers of the hopes we weave.
In the stillness, God's presence we meet,
Embracing the journey, our souls complete.

Through trials and triumphs, love ever near,
The journey unfolds with faith, not fear.
In the venture to light, we stand renewed,
With joy in our hearts and gratitude.

Together we wander, hand in hand,
In the embrace of grace, we take our stand.
In the warmth of faith, we shine so bright,
On a venture to the everlasting light.

The Sacred Dance of Our Lives

In the rhythm of prayer, we find our grace,
The sacred dance in this holy place.
Each step a blessing, each twirl a song,
In the dance of our lives, we all belong.

With hearts ablaze, we move as one,
A tapestry woven, the work begun.
Together we celebrate, hand in hand,
In the sacred dance, we make our stand.

Under the heavens, we sway and spin,
In the light of love, renewal begins.
Through joy and sorrow, we lift our voice,
In the sacred dance, we rejoice.

The beauty of movement, divine and true,
Guided by faith, in all that we do.
With every heartbeat, our spirits align,
In the dance of our lives, His love will shine.

As the day turns dusk, we gather near,
In the sacred dance, there's nothing to fear.
With gratitude in our hearts, we thrive,
In the sacred dance of our lives, we're alive.

Sacred Journeys

In paths of light we tread anew,
Heaven calls in whispers true.
Guided steps on sacred earth,
Each moment sings of holy worth.

With every prayer, the spirit soars,
In silence felt, our hearts implores.
Mountains high and valleys deep,
In faith's embrace, our souls we keep.

The dawn breaks with a gentle grace,
In every face, the divine trace.
A journey shared, we find our way,
In love's embrace, we choose to stay.

Through trials fierce and shadows cast,
The light of God shall hold us fast.
With every breath, we sing our song,
In sacred truth, we all belong.

So let us walk this blessed ground,
In every heartbeat, joy is found.
With grace as guide, our spirits rise,
In sacred journeys, love never dies.

In the Embrace of Faith

In quiet moments, grace descends,
The heart believes, the spirit mends.
With open arms, we seek the light,
In the embrace of faith, we ignite.

Each whispered prayer, a seed we sow,
In trusting hearts, the rivers flow.
Through trials faced and doubts cast wide,
We find our strength, with God as guide.

The sacred text, our lantern bright,
Illuminates the darkest night.
In fellowship, our voices rise,
In the embrace of hope, no disguise.

Anointed hands and loving deeds,
In every heart, a garden breeds.
Compassion flows, as mercy shines,
In the embrace of grace, love aligns.

So carry forth this sacred call,
In every step, uplift us all.
Together we stand, our spirits entwined,
In the embrace of faith, joy defined.

Tender Footprints on Holy Ground

With tender footprints, we walk the way,
On holy ground, where spirits sway.
Each step a prayer, a gentle plea,
In the childlike wonder, we find the key.

The sun-drenched morn, a promise bright,
Calls forth our hearts to share the light.
With grateful souls and loving hearts,
In sacred rhythms, life imparts.

Soft echoes of ancient lore,
Guide us onward, forevermore.
In nature's choir, a hymn resounds,
With tender footprints on holy grounds.

In valleys low, through struggles grim,
We lean on faith when lights grow dim.
With every tear, a strength unfolds,
In tender footprints, the story holds.

So let us walk with love's embrace,
On holy ground, in sacred space.
With open hearts and souls aligned,
In tender footprints, peace we find.

The Pilgrim's Solace

O weary traveler, find your rest,
In faith's embrace, you are truly blessed.
With every step, your soul takes flight,
The pilgrim's solace, a guiding light.

Through winding paths and shadowed lanes,
The gentle voice of love remains.
In every trial, a lesson learned,
The fire of hope within us burns.

In simple moments, grace unfolds,
In quiet places, the spirit holds.
With open eyes, the truth we seek,
The pilgrim's solace, strong, not weak.

Each whispered story, a cherished part,
In every heart, a sacred art.
With gratitude, we lift our song,
The pilgrim's solace, where we belong.

So journey forth with courage bright,
In every shadow, seek the light.
The path may twist, yet love will lead,
The pilgrim's solace, our hearts freed.

Tender Breezes on the Boulevard of Love

In the stillness, hearts do meet,
Whispers carried on wings so sweet.
Every glance, a sacred dance,
Love blooms gently, given a chance.

Gentle breezes kiss the soul,
Filling the void, making us whole.
Underneath the sky's embrace,
We walk together, love our grace.

Each moment, a divine decree,
In your eyes, I find my plea.
Boundless joy, the spirit sings,
Within our hearts, eternity springs.

With every step, a prayer unfolds,
Stories shared, and truth beholds.
Light surrounds our chosen way,
In love's arms, we softly sway.

Let the boulevard lead us near,
To the promise we hold dear.
Tender breezes, love so bright,
Guiding us through the night.

The Call to Sacred Wanderings

In twilight's glow, the voice does call,
To wander forth, to rise, not fall.
Footsteps echo on paths unknown,
In sacred spaces, wisdom's sown.

Beneath the stars, our spirits soar,
Seeking the truth, forevermore.
Nature speaks in whispers clear,
Guiding us, is love sincere.

Each step a journey, heart in hand,
Through valleys deep, in sunlit land.
The world unfolds, a canvas bright,
To paint our dreams, to seek the light.

Let every journey be a prayer,
In every heartbeat, presence rare.
With open hearts, and willing souls,
We chase the call that makes us whole.

In sacred wanderings, we find grace,
The journey leads to love's embrace.
Together, we transcend the strife,
Embarking on a sacred life.

Starlit Paths of Divine Connection

Through the night, the stars align,
Guiding souls, your heart is mine.
In the quiet, our spirits blend,
On these paths, we start to mend.

Shadows dance in moonlight's glow,
Revealing truths we long to know.
Each twinkle speaks of love's pure grace,
In this vastness, we find our place.

Whispers echo in the still,
Hearts awakened, spirits fill.
Hand in hand, we walk the way,
In starlit dreams, together we stay.

Every step, a sacred trust,
Through trials faced, in hope we must.
Love's connection, a thread divine,
Binding hearts and souls, entwined.

In the tapestry of night's embrace,
We find the light of every trace.
Starlit paths, our spirits soar,
In the divine, forevermore.

Echoes of Righteous Soles

In the silence, whispers fade,
Each step we take, a vow we've made.
Resounding truth beneath our feet,
Echoes of love, our souls repeat.

Through valleys low, and mountains high,
We seek the light that draws us nigh.
With righteous soles, we walk in grace,
In every trial, we find our place.

Together, hearts in unity,
Finding strength in community.
Hand in hand, we forge ahead,
Echoes of faith, where spirits tread.

The road may twist, the path may bend,
Yet in love, we will transcend.
Together, we rise, we gently soar,
Echoing truth from shore to shore.

In the journey, we understand,
The grace that guides us, hand in hand.
With righteous soles, we seek to shine,
In every moment, love divine.

The Dance of Faith and Doubt

In shadows cast by light so bright,
Two souls entwined in sacred fight.
One whispers hope, the other fears,
In every prayer, both shed their tears.

Through valleys low and mountains high,
They seek the Truth beyond the sky.
With trembling hearts, they take their stance,
Embracing both the doubt and dance.

Faith lifts them up, then pulls them down,
In chains of grace, they wear a crown.
Each step a struggle, each breath a gift,
Together, in the silence, they drift.

In darkened nights, the stars will gleam,
Each guiding light, a gentle beam.
In every sorrow, in every shout,
They find their way through faith and doubt.

Through every storm, they learn to trust,
In both despair and holy dust.
Their hearts united, forever bound,
In the sacred dance, their peace is found.

Finding the Divine in Our Steps

In every heartbeat, the Divine we seek,
Through life's journey, gentle and meek.
With open eyes, we tread the ground,
In simple acts, the Holy is found.

On dusty roads where shadows play,
The Spirit whispers, guiding our way.
Each footstep echoes, a prayer in motion,
Unfolding love like a vast ocean.

Through laughter shared and tears we shed,
In moments tender, where angels tread.
We walk together, hand in hand,
In the sacred silence, we understand.

Through trials faced and joy embraced,
In every moment, His love is traced.
With faith as our compass, hope as our guide,
In every step, the Lord abides.

As we journey forth, let spirits rise,
May our steps lead us to joyful skies.
For in this dance of the flesh and soul,
We find the Divine, we become whole.

The Silent Language of the Soul

Beneath the words that often fail,
In silence, where the heart's unveiled.
We whisper prayers without a sound,
In stillness, sacred truths abound.

Through gentle gazes and tender sighs,
The soul speaks volumes, no need for lies.
In every heartbeat, a sacred call,
The silent language unites us all.

In deep reflection, we pause to see,
The threads that weave our destiny.
A quiet strength in Christ we find,
In the depths of love, we are refined.

Hope dances lightly in shadows cast,
In moments still, the die is cast.
The whispers linger, a holy grace,
In every quiet, we find our place.

Through eyes that shine with purest light,
In harmony, our souls take flight.
As we embrace the sacred way,
The silent language guides our day.

A Passage Through Grace

In every trial, there lies a gift,
A passage through the pain we sift.
With each wound stitched by love's embrace,
We find the power of holy grace.

Through valleys deep where shadows creep,
His light will guide us, strong and steep.
In every tear, a promise made,
In every moment, His love won't fade.

With hearts wide open, we find the way,
Embracing dawn, embracing day.
In whispered prayers, our spirits rise,
Through trials faced, we reach the skies.

In brokenness, we find our whole,
A journey deep into the soul.
With faith as water, love the flame,
In every step, we call His name.

Through storms we weather, through nights we roam,
The path of grace will lead us home.
With every breath, we find our strength,
In love's embrace, we go the length.

Milton Keynes UK
Ingram Content Group UK Ltd.
UKHW022224251124
451566UK00006B/113